# BOOK ANALYSIS

Written by Flore Beaugendre
Translated by Carly Probert

AF143864

# Jane Eyre

BY CHARLOTTE BRONTË

Bright
≡Summaries.com

# CHARLOTTE BRONTË

## BRITISH NOVELIST

- **Born in Thornton (England) in 1816**
- **Died in Haworth in 1855**
- **Notable works:**
  - *Jane Eyre* (1847), novel
  - *Shirley* (1849), novel
  - *The Professor* (1857, posthumous), novel

Born in 1816, Charlotte Brontë is considered to be one of the greatest English writers of the 19th century. She was born into a modest family from Yorkshire. After her mother's death in 1821, she was raised by her father, an educated pastor, with her brother and four sisters. In 1846, she and her sisters began to publish poems under male pseudonyms. Anne and Emily then published *Agnes Grey* and *Wuthering Heights* respectively, but Charlotte's first novel, *The Professor*, was rejected. In 1847 *Jane Eyre* was published and achieved great success, and was soon followed by *Shirley* (1849) and *Villette* (1853). The last survivor of the Brontë family, she died in 1855 shortly after her marriage.

# *JANE EYRE*

## A FICTITIOUS AUTOBIOGRAPHY: THE LIFE OF A WOMAN

- **Genre:** novel
- **Reference edition:** Brontë, C. (1864) *Jane Eyre*. New York: Carleton Publisher.
- **First edition:** 1847
- **Themes:** love, initiation, determination, friendship, mystery, women, revolt

*Jane Eyre* was published in 1847 under the male pseudonym of Currer Bell. The novel shocked audiences with its determined and unconventional heroine, but became considerably successful. In the form of a fictitious autobiography, it presents the story of Jane Eyre, a poor and unattractive young orphan who tries to find her place in a society that places little importance on women. She becomes a governess and defies convention by falling in love with her master, Mr. Rochester. *Jane Eyre* is an emblematic work of English literature, as shown by the number of TV and cinema adaptations that have arisen from the novel.

# SUMMARY

## CHAPTERS 1-4

Jane Eyre is 10 years old and has lived at Gateshead Hall with Mrs. Reed, her aunt by marriage, since the death of her parents and her uncle. Orphaned and poor, she is unwelcome and mistreated by her guardian and her cousins, including the cruel John Reed. After yet another argument with him, Jane is locked in the red room where she experiences hallucinations. Traumatized, the little girl is unhappy and isolated. Only the nurse, Bessie, feels any sympathy for her. Mrs. Reed soon decides to get rid of her rebellious niece by sending her to a boarding school run by Mr. Brocklehurst, a tyrannical pastor.

## CHAPTERS 5-10

Jane arrives at the austere school, Lowood, where she soon settles in, despite the many hardships. The superintendent, sweet Miss Temple, tries to improve the lives of the students. Jane befriends Helen Burns, an intelligent and pious girl. In the spring, the school experiences a typhus epidemic which claims the lives of half of the children. Helen dies in Jane's arms. After the disaster, Mr. Brocklehurst is accused of negligence and life improves for the residents. Jane quickly recounts the following eight years of her life, during which she studies and becomes a teacher at Lowood. At 18, she becomes tired of her monotonous existence and seeks a position as a governess, after which she is hired by Mrs. Fairfax at Thornfield Hall. Before her departure, she is visited by Bessie who informs her that her father's brother had been trying to find her.

## CHAPTERS 11-16

Jane Eyre is warmly welcomed by Mrs. Fairfax, the housekeeper, and meets her pupil, Adèle, a little 8-year-old French girl. Jane hears a demonic laugh coming from the third floor, but Mrs. Fairfax assures her that it is Grace Poole, a maid who is a little crazy. While walking one evening, she meets an injured horseman and offers him help. She discovers that the rider is Mr. Rochester, the owner of the estate. They gradually get to know each other and the man tells her his story.

One night, Jane hears the laughter again and realizes that someone has set fire to her master's room: she saves his life. She is convinced that Grace Poole was responsible for the mischief, but Mr. Rochester puts the event down to an accident. When Mr. Rochester is away for some time, Jane realizes that she has strong feelings for him.

## CHAPTERS 17-21

Mr. Rochester returns to Thornfield Hall with a group of aristocrat friends and forces Jane to join them. Uncomfortable, she observes the proximity between her master and Miss Blanche Ingram, a young woman of great beauty, but haughty and wealth-obsessed. During their stay, a Mr. Mason comes to join them. In the night, he is brutally attacked and Jane suspects Grace Poole. Later, the master tells the young governess the story of a man who repents an error he committed in his youth and has to overcome a social obstacle if he wants to live with the woman he loves. He is, of course, speaking about himself. Jane is called to Gateshead Hall by her dying aunt. Her aunt confides in Jane that she had made her father's brother, John Eyre, believe that Jane was dead when he announced that he wanted to adopt her and bequeath his fortune to her. She dies without reconciling with her niece.

## CHAPTERS 22-25

A month later, Jane returns to Thornfield Hall where she expresses her joy at being reunited with her master, despite the prospect of his marriage to Miss Ingram. One night, she finds Mr. Rochester in the garden: he tells her that he is going to marry his fiancée and that she must leave. When Jane shows her grief, he admits that he wanted to make her jealous and asks her to marry him. Despite her surprise, Jane accepts. The wedding is planned to take place four weeks later. Embarrassed by the way in which Mr. Rochester idealizes her and by his generosity, she decides to write to her uncle in order to feel that she is equal with regards to his fortune. She then experiences scary and animated dreams that seem to act as foreboding premonitions.

## CHAPTERS 26-28

When Jane and Rochester are about to marry at the church, a voice rises to reveal the existence of Rochester's first wife, who was locked up in Thornfield Hall. The marriage is cancelled and Rochester exposes his wife, Bertha, a dangerous madwoman who is kept on the third floor of the mansion. He recounts his past to Jane but, despite their love, she decides to run away, refusing to live as his mistress. For three days, she wanders like a hungry and ill beggar, rejected by all. She finally arrives at the home of a pastor, St. John Rivers, and his two sisters, who offer her shelter.

## CHAPTERS 29-32

Jane recovers living alongside the friendly Diana and Mary and the distant St. John. Yet, she refuses to tell them her story. St. John promises to find her work. After a month, the two sisters must return to their positions as governesses. The Rivers indifferently learn that their uncle John has died and disinherited them. Jane is assigned a teaching post in the village. She quickly realizes that St. John is in love with a young woman, Rosamund Oliver, but he chooses to ignore his love as he wants to become a missionary and leave for India. One evening, he notices something on a drawing of Jane's and mysteriously leaves the room.

## CHAPTERS 33-35

One evening, when it is snowing, St. John tells Jane the story of a young orphan that everyone is looking for as she is to inherit 20,000 pounds, left by her Uncle John Eyre. Jane, dumbfounded, admits that she is Jane Eyre. She then learns that St. John and his sisters are her first cousins, disinherited by their uncle from Madeira because of an old dispute. Pleased to have a family, she shares her inheritance with them. A few months later, Miss Oliver is married and St. John still wishes to leave for India, so he asks Jane to accompany him and be his wife, so as to assist him in his divine mission. Appalled by his coldness, she refuses his request. He then displays a huge contempt for her. Under the pressure, she is about to consent to this sacrifice, when she believes that she is hearing the voice of Rochester calling, breaking the hold of St. John.

## CHAPTERS 36-38

Jane immediately leaves for Thornfield. She finds the manor in devastation and learns that it was destroyed in a fire. Bertha, the cause of the tragedy, then committed suicide by jumping from the roof. Mr. Rochester, in his attempts to save the inhabitants of his manor, became blind and lost an arm that night. He now lives as a recluse in Ferndean, his property hidden in the forest. Jane finds him there; their love is unchanged. Despite his hesitation due to his disability, he asks her to marry him again. She accepts. They are married without witnesses and experience blissful happiness. Jane Eyre ends her story by saying that she has been married for ten years. Rochester regained his sight and they had children. Her cousins are married and St. John, still in the East, has devoted his body and soul to his mission, sacrificing his life for it.

# CHARACTER STUDY

Jane Eyre is the narrator and heroine of the novel, which she presents as her autobiography. She is the result of a marriage between the rich Miss Reed and Mr. Eyre, a low rank pastor, who both died when she was an infant. Orphaned and poor, she spends her childhood with her Aunt Reed, who hates her, then at the boarding school of Lowood: she therefore has a very difficult start to life.

Throughout the work, the author stresses her lack of beauty: she is described as small, frail and graceless, both by the narrator herself and by the other characters. But the banality of her appearance does not reflect her personality: "Jane Eyre [...] is made up of strange contrasts. She is shy but does not lack audacity; submissive, but guards her independence fiercely; naïve, but full of common sense" (Preface). At the boarding school, after a rebellious childhood, she is able to acquire qualities such as loyalty and generosity. However, beneath her reserved nature, she is also an exalted soul, capable of transgression and great passion. Her character evolves throughout the novel, with her integrity and principles constantly being challenged, leading her to nuance her code of conduct. While searching for the happiness of a home, Jane is on a perpetual quest for freedom – intellectual, financial and social – and, through this, she opposes the rigidity of Victorian society.

## MR. ROCHESTER

Edward Rochester, the youngest son of Mr. Rochester, is the rich heir to the Thornfield estate. He is aged between 35 and 40 and is also often described as ugly: "I traced the general points of middle height and considerable breadth of chest. He had a dark face, with stern features and a heavy brow" (Chapter 12).

Like Jane Eyre, he is full of contradictions: he is both tough and gentle, haughty and haunted by his mistakes. Passionate and whimsical, he attaches little importance to social conventions. His past is similar to that of the heroine: his parents were indifferent and he never had a real home. Mr. Rochester has had a chaotic life journey. He has travelled a lot and acted as a libertine. His fate is decided by the women in his life.

He had a destructive relationship with the French dancer Céline Varens, a flighty woman who is the mother of his presumed daughter, Adèle. His marriage to Bertha Mason condemned him to misery and prevents him from marrying his alter ego, the woman who can save him, Jane Eyre.

## ST. JOHN RIVERS

St. John Rivers is Jane's cousin. He is the young pastor of a small country town. The narrator describes him as: "tall, slender; his face riveted the eye; it was like a Greek face, very pure in outline [...]It is seldom, indeed, an English face comes so near the antique models as did his. [...] His eyes were large and blue" (Chapter 29). This young thirty-year-old man is driven by a burning ambition and is fully devoted to God. He devotes himself to a missionary destiny in India and sacrifices everything, including his feelings and those of others, to realize his project. He is cold and haughty, contemptuous of those who claim their humanity.

St. John is the antithesis of Rochester: St. John is pure and devoted to God, while Rochester only knows passion; the pastor has icy blue eyes while the master of Thornfield has a fiery look; the beauty of the first is a contrast to the ugliness of the other.

For Jane to marry St. John, it would mean abandoning passion for the benefit of spiritual principles, while a marriage to Rochester would mean abandoning morality for the sake of passion. The fact remains that Jane's young cousin is bland and ridiculous compared to the mysterious Rochester.

## BERTHA MASON

Bertha Mason is the daughter of English and Jamaican parents. Very beautiful during her youth, she seduced the young Rochester to whom she was destined because of her dowry. He married her without really knowing her and soon realized that she suffered from madness.

The reader can see her as a symbol of the imprisonment of marriage at a time when women were dominated by men and could not exist by themselves. It is indeed interesting to compare the episode where Jane is locked in the red room with the situation of Bertha in Thornfield. She also seems to serve as a warning to Jane, who faces the possibility of a union with the passionate and powerful Rochester with reluctance. Bertha Mason is the antithesis of Jane: she represents darkness and fury while Jane embodies light and softness; she expresses rage and fear while the young teacher represses her feelings and fears. However, one cannot fail to notice a parallel between the two women: both of them surrender to Rochester and both of them fail in marrying him.

# ANALYSIS

## THE INFLUENCE OF THE GOTHIC NOVEL

The Gothic novel is a literary genre born in England at the end of the eighteenth century. It is generally considered to have originated from the pen of Horace Walpole (British writer, 1717-1797), author of *The Castle of Otranto* (1764), as well as from the fashion craze for the past and Gothic architecture, both consequences of the Romantic Movement.

The Gothic novel is dotted with clichés: the plot unfolds in dark and shadowy places (e.g. castles, churches, etc.) and the situations faced by the characters are dominated by the mysterious and diabolical, by secrets of the past or even by an unbridled nature. The story therefore takes place in a supernatural atmosphere.

*Jane Eyre* includes the elements of this genre. Lowood, Moor House and Thornfield Hall are all isolated places where raging storms take place. Thornfield, like Gateshead Hall, is an old mansion, with a maze of dark and disturbing corridors where Rochester hides his secrets. There are also numerous stories of the narrator's dreams, which are often frightening and premonitory. All of these elements run through the novel, creating an atmosphere akin to the Gothic trend. Charlotte Brontë also introduces scenes that can be traced back directly to this genre, such as that of the red room, where little Jane believes she sees the ghost of her deceased uncle, an experience that will mark her forever, or the scene where she receives a nighttime visit from Bertha Mason, who she likens to a vampire: "Shall I tell you of what it reminded me? [...]Of the foul German spectre—the Vampyre" (Chapter 25). However, one can see that the author always provides an opportunity to find an explanation for these mysterious events: the light that appears on the wall of the red room is a reflection from the lantern, the vampire is actually Rochester's first wife, etc. Only at the end of the work are we left with an unanswered question: the mystery of Rochester's call heard by Jane at Moor House is confirmed and there is no rational justification. The reader is therefore left to interpret this amazing fact.

Thus, *Jane Eyre* is clearly a descendant of the Gothic trend, which was still prevalent at the time of Charlotte Brontë's writing. However, the author does not seek to write a novel of this kind: she mainly uses the inherent Gothic characteristics to maintain the suspense and heighten the romance inherent to the plot.

## A FEMINIST WORK

*Jane Eyre* creates an image of the condition of women that is not without its feminist connotations. In Victorian society in the middle of the nineteenth century, women were not in a position to achieve freedom and independence. However, the quest for both seems to have plagued the heroine since her childhood. She demonstrates an independence of mind by constructing her own opinions. She also wants to free herself of social oppression by possessing her own fortune, allowing her to be an equal to Rochester and to consider him as her husband as opposed to her master. She rises against the conventional ideas that label women as inferior to men. In chapter 12, there is one paragraph that is particularly daring and modern for its time and calls for gender equality:

> "Women are supposed to be very calm generally: but women feel just as men feel; they need exercise for their faculties, and a field for their efforts, as much as their brothers do; they suffer from too rigid a restraint, too absolute a stagnation, precisely as men would suffer; and it is narrow-minded in their more privileged fellow-creatures to say that they ought to confine themselves to making puddings and knitting stockings, to playing on the piano and embroidering bags. It is thoughtless to condemn them, or laugh at them, if they seek to do more or learn more than custom has pronounced necessary for their sex" (Chapter 12).

Jane Eyre must constantly fight to escape male oppression, whether from the contemptuous Mr. Brocklehurst who seeks to debase her, from St. John Rivers who wants to trap her in a loveless marriage that goes against her very nature, or from Mr. Rochester, each of these men being misogynistic. She also commits two acts towards Rochester that seem particularly feminist: the first when she refuses to accept the jewelry and beautiful dresses, as she believes he wishes to make her a ceremonial object by doing this, and the second when she leaves him, refusing to be only his mistress and never being able to achieve an equal status. Her courage and ability to abandon comfort and safety prove how high she holds her dignity and integrity, and one cannot be surprised by the fact that this disregard of social norms shocked Charlotte Brontë's contemporaries. We should, however, note that the much desired independence of the heroine comes from a man, her uncle. The novel ends with a paradoxical loop: the young Jane claims freedom of mind and must escape from the masculine characters who block her path, but it is nonetheless through one of these characters that she is able to achieve her desires and return to the man she loves.

The claims of Jane Eyre are therefore symbolic and seem natural for the heroine. They are, in a sense, a taster of feminism, the development of which is contemporary to the writing of the novel. Charlotte Maurat summarizes the momentum of the author: "For the first time, Charlotte Brontë, ahead of her time, advocates in *Jane Eyre* the social emancipation of women. The awareness and the perception of her rights were simply proof of a clear-sighted spirit, a proud soul" (Preface).

## RELIGION

Throughout the novel, the narrator is torn between the pursuit of happiness and her moral and religious duties, which were ingrained in her education. The theme of religion is crucial in *Jane Eyre*. It is embodied by three characters encountered by the heroine, three models to which she cannot conform. Reverend Brocklehurst is the first representative of God encountered by the reader. He displays austerity and rigid principles: he inflicts hardship on his residents to teach them about humility, drawing from Evangelical Protestantism. His precepts are devoid of charity, compassion and sincerity. Although he professes starkness in others, he encourages vanity and luxury in his own home. Evidently, he uses religion to establish authority over his flock. The contrast of the Brocklehurst tyrannical methods with the behavior of Helen Burns is striking. Jane's friend's faith is boundless and devoid of hypocrisy. She is tolerant and submissive to the extreme, taking each injustice in her stride as a sign of divine will. She embodies the following biblical principle: "If anyone strikes you on the cheek, offer the other also". The young Helen only envisages happiness in Paradise. St. John Rivers, meanwhile, offers a cold and ambitious vision of religion, completely devoted to his ideals at the expense of all sense and human value. He advocates absolute sacrifice and is unable to feel compassion. Robert de Traz expresses the negative aspect of his character: "Painting a saint and showing the other side to his holiness is the almost impossible purpose of Charlotte, yet one that is beautifully executed" (DE TRAZ R., *La famille Brontë*, Paris, Albin Michel, 1939, p. 135).

Jane cannot be satisfied with these three extremist and caricature conceptions of faith, since they do not fit her own personality, but she remains very religious. She manages to build her own conception of religion, in which she sees a way to curb immoderate passions and arrive at full self-knowledge. By comparing the different practices of the characters, Charlotte Brontë offers a vehement satire of the hypocrisy and vanity of certain representatives of God, as embodied by Mr. Brocklehurst.

# FURTHER REFLECTION

## SOME QUESTIONS TO THINK ABOUT...

- In what way can we view *Jane Eyre* as a novel of learning?
- What are the influences of romanticism on the novel?
- Charlotte Brontë lends some autobiographical elements to her main characters. What are they? Can we therefore regard this work as an autobiographical account?
- Do you think Jane Eyre is a reliable narrator? Or, does Charlotte Brontë invite the reader to read between the lines? Explain your answer.
- Mr. Rochester and Jane Eyre are both described as being devoid of beauty. In your opinion, what is revealed by this insistence on their ungainly physique?
- The theme of the substitute mother is recurrent in the work. How does it manifest itself?
- The female characters are numerous in *Jane Eyre*. Explain how each of them offers a different representation of women.
- Highlight the occurrences of a contrast between fire and ice. In your opinion, what does this symbolize?
- The oppression of social classes and the transgression of conventions are important themes in the novel. Analyze how Charlotte Brontë tackles this delicate subject.
- Analyze the episode of the red room. How can this be interpreted and what is its role in the work?
- Charlotte Brontë is being somewhat chauvinistic in her novel. Expand this theory by analyzing the characters of Céline Varens and Adèle.

*We want to hear from you!*
*Leave a comment on your online library*
*and share your favourite books on social media!*

# FURTHER READING

## REFERENCE EDITION

- Brontë, C. (1864) *Jane Eyre*. New York: Carleton Publisher.

## REFERENCE STUDIES

- De Traz, R. (1939) *La famille Brontë*. Paris: Albin Michel.

## ADAPTATIONS

- *Jane Eyre*. (1944) [Film]. Robert Stevenson. Dir. USA: Twentieth Century Fox Film Corporation.
- *Jane Eyre*. (1996) [Film]. Franco Zeffirelli. Dir. France: Cineritino S.r.L.
- *Jane Eyre*. (2011) [Film]. Cary Joji Fukunaga. Dir. UK/USA: Focus Features.